ENCYCLOPÆDIA
Britannica®

Animals

pil
Publications International, Ltd.

Get the App!

This book is enhanced by an app that can be downloaded from the App Store or Google Play*. Apps are available to download at no cost. Once you've downloaded the app to your smartphone**, use the QR code found on page 3 of this book to access an immersive, 360° virtual reality environment. Then slide the phone into the VR viewer and you're ready to go.

Compatible Operating Systems

- Android 4.1 (JellyBean) or later

- iOS 8.0 or later

Compatible Phones

Removing your device from its case may provide a better fit in the viewer. If your smartphone meets the above operating system requirements and has gyroscope functionality it should support GoogleVR. Publications International, Ltd. has developed and tested this software with the following devices:

- Google Nexus 5, Google Nexus 5X, Google Nexus 6P, Google Pixel

- Apple iPhone 6, Apple iPhone 6S, Apple iPhone 6 Plus, Apple iPhone 6S Plus, Apple iPhone 7, Apple iPhone 7 Plus

- Samsung Galaxy S5, Samsung Galaxy S5 Active, Samsung Galaxy S5 Sport, Samsung Galaxy S6, Samsung Galaxy S6 edge, Samsung Galaxy S6 edge +, Samsung Galaxy Note 4, Samsung Galaxy Note edge, Samsung Galaxy S7, Samsung Galaxy S7 edge, Samsung Galaxy Note 5, Samsung Galaxy S8

Caution

The viewer should not be exposed to moisture or extreme temperatures. The viewer is not water resistant. It is potentially combustible if the lenses are left facing a strong light source.

Apple, the Apple logo and iPhone are trademarks of Apple Inc., registered in the U.S. and other countries. App Store is a service mark of Apple Inc., registered in the U.S. and other countries. Google Play and the Google Play logo are trademarks of Google Inc. Nexus and Pixel are trademarks of Google Inc. Samsung, Galaxy and Galaxy Note are trademarks of Samsung Electronics Co. Ltd.

 **Publications International, Ltd.**

For inquiries email: customer_service@pubint.com

ISBN: 978-1-64030-168-9

Manufactured in China.

8 7 6 5 4 3 2 1

*We reserve the right to terminate the apps.
**Smartphone not included. Standard data rates may apply to download. Once downloaded, the app does not use data or require wifi access.

ANIMALS
INSTRUCTIONS

1 Carefully remove the viewer from the book along the perforated edge. Gently push each side of the viewer inward. Then push the front of the viewer into place.

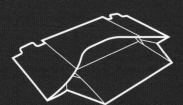 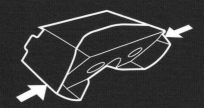 

2 Download PI VR Animals, available on the App Store or Google Play. Direct links to the store locations are found at: pilbooks.com/PIVRAnimals.

3 Launch the app. If you are asked to calibrate the viewer, go to page 64 and follow the instructions found there. If asked, allow the app to take photos/videos.

4 When the app loads, you will be prompted to scan the QR code found to the right to verify your possession of this book.

5 You will see a double image of a savannah landscape on your phone. Slide your smartphone into the front compartment of the VR viewer. The line between the two images should line up with the seam found on the bottom of the viewer, between the two lenses. If your screen seems blurry, make sure the smartphone is aligned precisely with the center of the viewer. Adjusting the phone left or right a few millimeters can make a big difference. The tilt of the viewer and the phone can also affect how the screen looks to you.

6 Look around to explore! PI VR Animals does not require a lever or remote control. You control each interaction with your gaze. When you see a loading circle, keep your gaze focused until it loads fully to access videos, slideshows, and games.

Loading

7 Gaze at the X to close out of video, slideshow, or game screens.

Exit

CONTENTS

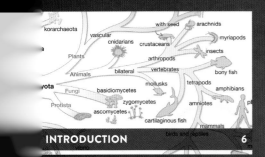

INTRODUCTION

Living things are divided into three main groups called domains. Two domains, Bacteria and Archaea, are each made up of single-celled organisms. A third domain, Eukarya, includes not only single-celled algae and protozoa but also animals and other multicellular organisms. Animals form the largest group within the Eukarya. They range from very simple invertebrates, such as sponges, to highly complex mammals, such as whales, monkeys, and humans.

Some of the most familiar animals, such as dogs, birds, frogs, and fish, have a backbone and a central nervous system. They are called vertebrates, meaning animals with spinal columns, or backbones. Animals without backbones are called invertebrates and include arthropods, worms, mollusks, and many other groups.

In this book, we'll explore the many kinds of animal life, from the simplest to the very complex.

FIVE FAST FACTS

1 Scientists estimate that there may be more than 10 million different species, or kinds, of animals on Earth today.

2 About 1.3 million species have been identified to date, and new species are continually being discovered.

3 Animals evolved in the seas. They moved into fresh water and onto land more than 350 million years ago.

4 Most animals move freely from place to place and can sense their surroundings; that is, they can taste, smell, hear, see, and touch. Certain simple animals, such as the corals and barnacles, spend most of their lives fastened to one spot, but when they are young they are able to swim freely.

5 All animals must take in oxygen in order to change food into a form that the body can use.

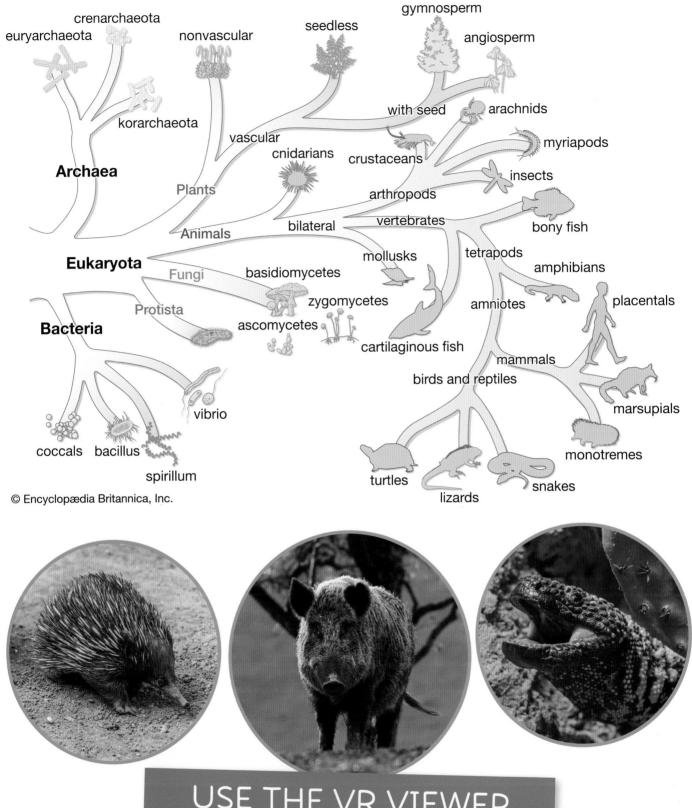

euryarchaeota
crenarchaeota
korarchaeota

Archaea

nonvascular
seedless
gymnosperm
angiosperm

vascular
Plants
cnidarians
with seed
arachnids
crustaceans
myriapods
insects
arthropods
vertebrates
bony fish
Animals
bilateral
Eukaryota
mollusks
tetrapods
Fungi
basidiomycetes
amphibians
zygomycetes
Protista
ascomycetes
amniotes
placentals
Bacteria
cartilaginous fish
mammals
birds and reptiles
marsupials
vibrio
monotremes
coccals bacillus
turtles
lizards
snakes
spirillum

© Encyclopædia Britannica, Inc.

USE THE VR VIEWER AND ASSOCIATED APP

Enhance your experience by using the app! Put your smartphone in the VR viewer and you'll be able to visit the African savannah, find out more about animal camouflage, play a game, and more!

INVERTEBRATES

Most of the more than one million animal species known to exist on Earth are invertebrates, or animals without backbones. The absence of a backbone is the main trait that distinguishes invertebrates from vertebrates, or animals with backbones. Apart from the absence of a backbone, invertebrate groups have little in common; rather, they comprise a highly diverse and largely unrelated group of animals. Lobsters, insects, spiders, worms, jellyfish, clams, crabs, sea stars, sea urchins, and sponges are but a few examples of invertebrates.

In form and function, invertebrates and vertebrates share many characteristics. For example, members of both groups may have complex eyes, gills, poison defense mechanisms, and hemoglobin. Yet some invertebrates have characteristics not found in vertebrates. Radial symmetry, in which the body shape is roughly circular with the body parts equally spaced, and skeletons that are on the outside of the body are exclusive to certain invertebrate groups.

The sea cucumber is an example of radial symmetry.

The millipede is an arthropod.

Sea stars are echinoderms.

A VARIETY OF BODIES

The invertebrate animals can be grouped according to their features. Many of them, such as worms, have soft bodies. Corals, jellyfish, and sea anemones are invertebrates that have stinging tentacles. Mollusks have soft bodies as well, but most also have a thick outside shell. Oysters and snails are mollusks.

Some invertebrates have a tough, spiny skin that protects their bodies. These invertebrates are called echinoderms. Sea stars and sea urchins are examples of echinoderms.

Other invertebrates have a hard outside covering on their bodies called an exoskeleton. These invertebrates are called arthropods. Arthropods include insects, spiders, centipedes, millipedes, and crustaceans such as lobsters and crabs.

FIVE FAST FACTS

1 More than 90 percent of all living animal species are invertebrates.

2 More than two dozen phyla (plural of phylum, or major group) of living invertebrates, plus many extinct forms, are recognized.

3 A few invertebrate phyla have only a few known species, but some—such as the arthropods—have thousands of living representatives.

4 The sponges (phylum Porifera), among the simplest of the invertebrate groups, are best described as a mass of specialized cells that carry out bodily functions.

5 The simplest animals are invertebrates.

WORMS

Adult animals that have soft, elongated, often tubelike bodies and that lack backbones are commonly called worms. Worms are so different from one another that zoologists do not classify them together in a single group; they place them in about a dozen different and often unrelated taxonomic groups called phyla.

Worms play a major role in virtually all ecosystems. Some terrestrial worms condition the soil. Many worms are parasites of plants and animals, including humans. Many free-living, or nonparasitic, worms form an important link in food chains.

An earthworm.

WORM CHARACTERISTICS

All worms are bilaterally symmetrical, meaning that the two sides of their bodies are identical. They lack scales and true limbs, though they may have appendages such as fins and bristles. Many worms have sense organs to detect chemical changes in their environments, and some have light-sensing organs.

Some worms are extremely mobile; they may burrow, crawl, or swim. Other worms are sedentary and live in burrows or tubes that they have built for themselves. Some worms are scavengers, others are carnivorous predators, and still others are totally parasitic.

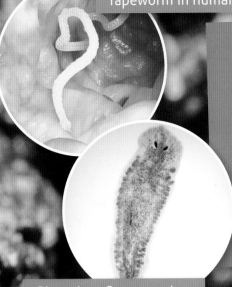

Tapeworm in human intestine.

Planaria, a flatworm that can regenerate parts.

FAST FACTS ABOUT FLATWORMS

- The flatworms (phylum Platyhelminthes) comprise more than 10,000 flat, elongate species.

- The three taxonomic classes in the phylum are the free-living (nonparasitic) flatworms, the flukes, and the tapeworms.

- Many flatworms have cilia (movable, bristlelike structures) on their outer surface that aid in locomotion and feeding.

FAST FACTS ABOUT SEGMENTED WORMS

- The segmented worms (phylum Annelida) consist of about 9,000 species of free-living and parasitic forms.

- The two classes of segmented worms that are most familiar include the earthworms and leeches. Most segmented worms, however, are ocean forms that are not familiar to most people.

- The segmented worms possess a well-developed nervous system with concentrations of nerve cells called ganglia that are considered primitive brains.

FAST FACTS ABOUT ROUNDWORMS

- Roundworms, which make up the phylum Nematoda, are among the most abundant multicellular animals in the world. Millions can be found in a square meter of garden soil or ocean mud.

- There are more than 10,000 known species.

- Many roundworms are parasitic and nearly every major group of plants and animals is capable of being infested by at least one species.

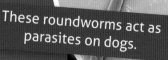

These roundworms act as parasites on dogs.

ARTHROPODS

Arthropods are animals that have a hard outer shell called an exoskeleton that supports and protects the animal's soft body. Arthropods are scientifically classified as members of the phylum Arthropoda, the largest phylum in the animal kingdom. Examples of arthropods include such familiar forms as lobsters, crabs, spiders, ticks and mites, insects, and centipedes and millipedes.

ABOUT THE EXOSKELETON

The exoskeleton of arthropods is composed of a substance called chitin, which is hard and unbendable. This exoskeleton is secreted by the underlying epidermis (which corresponds to the skin of other animals). The body is usually segmented, and the segments bear paired, jointed appendages. These can range from three pairs in many insects to about 200 pairs in some millipedes.

Dust mites are arthropods.

FIVE FAST FACTS

① About 84 percent of all known species of animals are members of this phylum.

② About one million arthropod species have been described, of which most are insects. This number, however, may be only a fraction of the total.

③ Arthropods are found in every habitat on Earth.

④ Most arthropods are small animals. Land-dwelling types range in size from mites that measure less than 0.01 inch (0.25 millimeter) in length to the giant walkingstick (*Pharnacia serratipes*), which can reach a length of 13 inches (33 centimeters).

⑤ Some arthropods living in water, however, are able to attain substantial sizes, because their bodies are supported in part by the surrounding water.

MOLTING

Because the exoskeleton is hard and rigid, it does not grow with the animal. Therefore, arthropods go through a series of molts. Molting involves the shedding of the old exoskeleton and the forming of a new one. The old skeleton splits along specific lines characteristic of the group, and the animal pulls out of the old skeleton as from a suit of clothes. The old skeleton is usually abandoned, but in some species it is eaten. The new exoskeleton, when first produced, is soft and flexible, leaving the animal vulnerable to both predators and environmental changes.

A cicada molting.

DANGEROUS ARTHROPODS?

A number of carnivorous arthropods, notably spiders, scorpions, and centipedes, capture prey with poison, which is usually delivered with a pair of appendages; scorpions use a single stinger at the tip of the tail. In spiders, the poison is introduced through a pair of fangs flanking the mouth, and in centipedes the poison claws lie beneath the head. Few of these species have a venom that is fatal to humans.

A venomous centipede.

An emperor scorpion.

INSECTS

The world's most abundant creatures are the insects, whose known species outnumber all the other animals and the plants combined. Insects have been so successful in their fight for life that they are sometimes described as the human race's closest rivals for domination of the Earth. Entomologists, the scientists who study insects, have named almost 1,000,000 species—perhaps less than one third of the total number.

Insects thrive in almost any habitat where life is possible. Some are found only in the Arctic regions, and some live only in deserts. Others thrive only in fresh water or only in brackish water. Many species of insects are able to tolerate both freezing and tropical temperatures. Such hardy species are often found to range widely over the Earth. Few insects, however, inhabit marine environments. Small size, relatively minor food requirements, and rapid reproduction have all aided in perpetuating the many species of insects.

FIVE FAST FACTS

1 The oldest fossils of ancestral insect forms are believed to be some 350 million years old.

2 There are also fossil records, from later eras, of highly developed forms very similar to the mayflies, cockroaches, and dragonflies now in existence. Some ancient insects were truly huge; dragonflies, for example, had a wingspread of 2 feet (0.61 meter) or more.

3 As vectors, or transmitting agents, of disease organisms, insects have caused more deaths and have inflicted greater misery and hardship on humankind than all the wars of history.

4 Most insects are herbivorous—that is, they feed on plants. Virtually every part of a plant, from the flower to the root, is vulnerable to their attack.

5 Numerous species of plants depend upon insects to pollinate them. In visiting flowers for nectar, insects carry pollen from one flower to the pistil of another. In this way they fertilize the plant and enable it to make seeds. Without insects there would be no orchard fruits or berries. Tomatoes, peas, onions, cabbages, and many other vegetables would not exist.

A horsefly's compound eyes.

A honeybee collects nectar.

Fossilized insects in amber.

INSECT ANATOMY

Insects are distinguished from other members of the animal kingdom by having six legs; one pair of antennae; a ringed, or segmented, body; and three well-defined body regions: the head, the thorax, and the abdomen. The head usually is composed of mouthparts, a single pair of antennae, and compound eyes, which in some species have color vision. Compound eyes are made up of a compact network of single lenses that allows more precise detection of shapes and movements than do simple eyes. The thorax comprises three distinct segments, each bearing a pair of legs. Wings are usually present and are also located on the thorax. The abdomen, composed of several segments, houses the lower portion of the digestive tract and the reproductive organs.

VERTEBRATES

Animals with backbones are called vertebrates. They comprise one of the best-known groups of animals and include fishes, amphibians, reptiles, birds, and mammals, including humans. Vertebrates are members of the subphylum Vertebrata, which is part of the phylum Chordata.

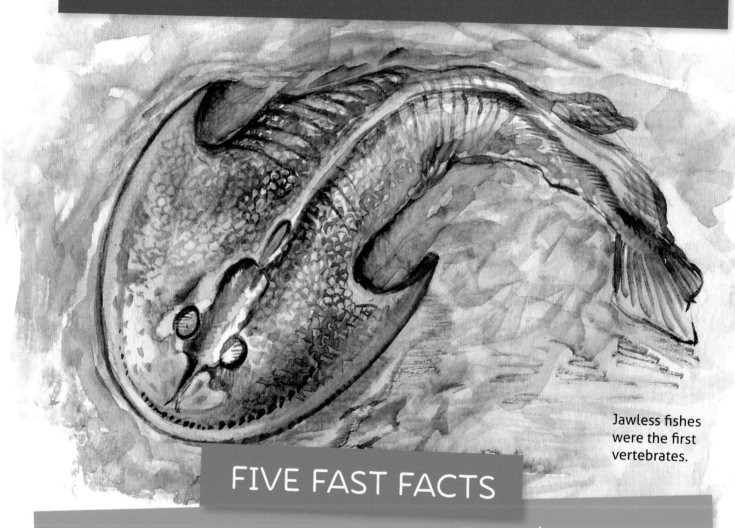

Jawless fishes were the first vertebrates.

FIVE FAST FACTS

1 The earliest vertebrates were marine, or ocean-dwelling, organisms.

2 Over millions of years, some early marine vertebrates that were adapted to breathe air and move across land were able to colonize terrestrial, or land, habitats.

3 There are approximately 45,000 living species of vertebrates.

4 Vertebrates inhabit every region on Earth except for the ice packs of the North Pole and the interiors of Antarctica and Greenland.

5 Vertebrates range in size from the tiniest fishes to the elephants and the whales, the largest animals ever to have existed.

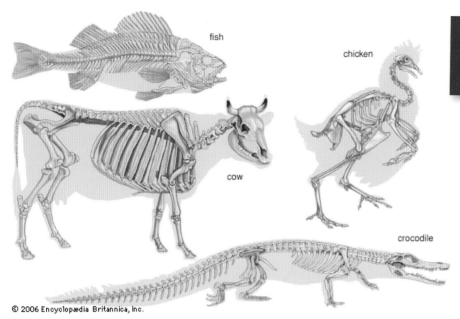

fish

chicken

cow

crocodile

© 2006 Encyclopædia Britannica, Inc.

Vertebrates

reptiles

mammals

birds

whale

fishes

groundhog

amphibians

human

© 2006 Encyclopædia Britannica, Inc.

ANIMALS WITH BACKBONES

The presence of a hollow, jointed backbone is the main feature that distinguishes vertebrates from invertebrates (animals that lack a backbone). The backbone is composed of specialized interconnected bones called vertebrae. The vertebrae surround and protect the spinal cord, which connects to the brain, thus forming the central nervous system. The brain is enclosed within a skull, forming the head. Vertebrates are also characterized by an internal skeleton that supports the body.

FISHES VS. TETRAPODS

The vertebrates can be divided broadly into two main groups based on the presence or absence of limbs: the fishes, which lack limbs, and the tetrapods. Each group is further subdivided into categories based on common key features.

The fishes are a highly diverse group but share four common characteristics: they lack limbs, live in water, take in oxygen from the water through gills, and are ectothermic, or cold-blooded, meaning they cannot regulate their internal body temperature.

Tetrapods are vertebrates with four limbs. The word tetrapod means "four feet." The tetrapods are divided into four major groups: amphibians, reptiles, birds, and mammals. The limbs are absent or greatly reduced in size in some tetrapods, such as snakes and whales. Most tetrapods are terrestrial; however, some groups adapted to a life spent in or near water.

AMPHIBIANS

Four hundred million years ago the most advanced forms of life on Earth, the fishes, lived in the water. Plants and insects alone occupied the land until the appearance of the amphibians more than 350 million years ago. Almost all amphibians have features that fall between those of fishes and those of reptiles. The most commonly known amphibians are frogs, toads, and salamanders. Although most have changed very little since they first began to breathe on land, some of the early amphibians were the ancestors of today's reptiles, birds, and mammals.

Red poison dart frog.

ON LAND AND IN WATER

The word *amphibian* comes from the Greek *amphi*, meaning "both," and *bios*, meaning "life." It describes cold-blooded animals with backbones that pass their lives both in fresh water and on land. Because amphibians live in water and on land, their natural environments are shores, ponds, marshes, swamps, and low-lying meadows.

FIVE FAST FACTS

1 There are more than 6,500 existing species of amphibians.

2 Amphibians are distributed throughout the world, except in regions covered with snow all year long.

3 The skin's protective properties include the ability to change color so that the animal can hide when an enemy is nearby. Certain cells under the skin alter the color so that the amphibian can blend into its surroundings.

4 Sometimes parts of the skin become brightly colored. The amphibian displays these colors to enemies to warn them to keep away.

5 Frogs and toads have a strong sense of location. When taken from their territories or breeding grounds, they can find their way back by smell and instinctively by the position of the stars.

Poison dart frog.

Natterjack toad.

Orange strawberry poison dart frog.

AMPHIBIAN SKIN

The moist, supple skin of most amphibians provides protection and absorbs water and oxygen. The upper skin layer, called the epidermis, is regularly shed in a process called molting. The skin usually comes off in one piece and is then eaten by the animal.

The lower skin layer, called the dermis, of the typical amphibian often includes mucous and poison glands. The mucous glands help provide essential moisture to the body. The protective poison glands are quite often located in different places on different species—by the ears in certain toads, and behind the eyes of salamanders. These glands produce poisons that are toxic to natural enemies, such as birds and small mammals, but that rarely harm humans.

METAMORPHOSIS

Most amphibians begin their lives in the water as tadpoles, or larvae, which breathe by means of external gills instead of lungs. At first the tadpole has no definite shape, and no tail can be seen. The mouth is a V-shaped sucker on the underside of the body. As the head grows, a round mouth with a horny rim develops. At the same time, the tadpole grows a flat, finlike tail. The tiny creature later changes to adult form and breathes at least partly through lungs. This transformation process is called metamorphosis. The larval stage lasts from several weeks to one year, depending on the particular species and upon environmental factors such as temperature and humidity. Certain species of amphibians, particularly among the salamanders, remain in larval form all their lives. This phenomenon is called neoteny.

Amphibians are divided into three orders: Anura, or Salientia; Urodela, or Caudata; and Apoda, or Gymnophiona.

THREE ORDERS

ANURA

The anurans include true frogs, tree frogs, and toads. True frogs have long hind legs and well-developed swimming and leaping powers. Tree frogs have suction pads on their fingers and toes so that they can hold on to smooth surfaces. Toads have shorter legs than frogs, and their skin has a warty appearance.

All anurans begin life as tadpoles, tiny fishlike larvae with tails and gills. As they become adults, they lose their tails and gills and develop hind legs suitable for jumping. There are more frogs than any other kind of amphibian.

Couch's Spadefoot toad.

URODELA

The urodeles are the tailed amphibians. All of them resemble the most numerous members of this order—the salamanders. Basically animals of the Northern Hemisphere, urodeles live in or near streams, and are sometimes found under rocks and logs. They have long tails, poorly developed legs, and smooth, moist skin. The giant salamander of Japan is the largest of all amphibians. It grows to a length of about 5 feet (1.5 meters).

Fire salamander.

APODA

The gymnophions, or caecilians, are the least understood and most rarely seen amphibians. They are blind and limbless, with long, slender bodies, like worms or snakes. Buried in a pit near each useless eye is a protruding tentacle. The animal uses this organ to feel its way about. They are found throughout the tropics, mostly in South America, Africa, and islands of the Indian Ocean. Their scales are buried in their skin.

Caecilian.

Komodo dragon.

REPTILES

According to fossil records, reptiles first appeared on Earth more than 300 million years ago. In fact, birds and mammals evolved from reptilian ancestors. Reptiles are distinguished from other vertebrates by the fact that they have dry scales covering their bodies. Reptiles are further distinguished from vertebrates lower on the evolutionary scale by their ability to perform internal fertilization, whereby the male places sperm inside the female. The scales of reptiles differ in structure and development from those of fish, and, unlike amphibians, reptiles have few or no glands present in their skin. Unlike birds and mammals, which maintain relatively constant internal temperatures, the body temperature of reptiles is directly affected by the temperature of the reptiles' surroundings. The brains of reptiles are proportionally much smaller than those of similar-sized mammals.

FIVE FAST FACTS

1 Modern reptiles range in size from species of tiny snakes and lizards with lengths of less than 2 inches (5 centimeters) to crocodiles, pythons, and anacondas that grow to more than 30 feet (9 meters) long.

2 The largest lizard is the Komodo dragon, which reaches a length of more than 10 feet (3 meters).

3 Reptiles replace their scales throughout their lifetimes. For some species, shedding is continual, while for others it is a seasonal occurrence. Snakes shed all of their scales at once. Lizards, crocodilians, and turtles shed their scales individually or in patches.

4 During cold weather, most reptiles hibernate. Some reptiles undergo a hibernation-like phase called estivation, in which they become dormant during the hot, dry part of the summer.

5 The life spans of some reptiles are among the longest known for any vertebrates. Many species of reptiles have lived for more than 20 years in zoos, and individuals of some species of turtles have been known to live for more than 150 years.

A snake shedding.

AMNIOTIC EGGS

Reptiles produce amniotic eggs, which differ from those of amphibians by having special membranes and a shell that help prevent the embryo from drying up in a terrestrial environment where moisture levels may be low. It was owing largely to their amniotic eggs that reptiles became the first vertebrates to adapt completely to life on land.

TYPES OF REPTILES

There were once about 16 orders in this class. Today the class includes only four: the turtles, the crocodilians, the beaked reptiles, and the snakes and lizards.

TURTLES

Turtles exist throughout the world except in the coldest climates. The greatest abundance and variety of turtles are found in temperate regions. Most turtles live in freshwater habitats, but many spend time on land, either traveling between bodies of water or hibernating. The females come ashore during warm months to lay eggs. The tortoises are strictly land dwelling, and many inhabit deserts or other arid environments.

CROCODILIANS

The order Crocodilia—the alligators and crocodiles—consists of fewer than two dozen, mostly tropical, species of similar appearance and habits. The American and Chinese alligators are the only exclusively Temperate Zone species. Most crocodilians live in freshwater habitats, though some venture into salt water. All alligators and crocodiles are capable of at least short overland excursions.

The order of beaked reptiles, Rhynchocephalia, contains a single living family with only one species, the tuatara. Lizardlike animals with a scaly crest, the tuataras are confined to a few rocky islands of New Zealand. They live in underground burrows during the day and emerge to feed at night. They differ from most reptiles in that they are able to tolerate cold temperatures.

TUATARAS

Gila monster.

Most living reptiles belong to the order Squamata, which includes more than 2,500 species of snakes (suborder Serpentes) and more than 3,000 species of lizards (suborder Sauria). Squamates occur in greatest numbers in the tropics, but many snakes and lizards occur in the higher temperate regions, and a few range near or above the Arctic Circle.

Squamates occupy a wide range of habitats. Some sea snakes are permanent residents of warm seas, and many species of tropical snakes and lizards are almost exclusively tree dwelling. Deserts, freshwater aquatic habitats, and even urban areas are inhabited by various species of squamates.

The only venomous lizards in the world (family Helodermatidae) are the Gila monster of the southwestern United States and the Mexican beaded lizard of northern Mexico.

SNAKES AND LIZARDS

BIRDS

Just exactly what is a bird? Perhaps you would say that a bird is an animal that flies. But butterflies, which are insects, and bats, which are mammals, also fly. Some birds, on the other hand, do not fly at all. The ostrich, the emu, and the kiwi run very fast. The penguin swims with its short paddlelike wings. None of them can fly.

All birds, however, have feathers, which no other living animal has, though paleontologists have found fossilized remains of a few dinosaurs and other reptiles—probably the ancestors of birds—that appear to have had feathers. Birds are feathered, warm-blooded animals with backbones. They have two legs. Whether they fly or not, all have a pair of wings corresponding to the arms or the front legs of many other animals. A beak takes the place of a jaw with teeth. All birds lay eggs. Most of them build a nest in which they care for the eggs and the young birds.

A hovering bird of prey.

The flightless kiwi.

A swan.

FIVE FAST FACTS

1 Today there are about 30,000 known varieties of birds.

2 The eyesight of birds is far keener than that of human beings. An American kestrel hovering 100 feet (30 meters) above a field can spot a grasshopper and drop directly on it, keeping it in focus all the way to the ground.

3 Besides the upper and lower eyelids, birds have a third eyelid—called the nictitating membrane. It is transparent and moves from side to side instead of up and down. It keeps the eye moist and protects it from dust.

4 The neck of a bird moves more freely than that of any other animal. This is because it has more vertebrae, or sections of the backbone. The sparrow has 14 vertebrae in its neck. A giraffe or a human has only seven.

5 A bird's heart beats faster than a human heart, and birds breathe more rapidly than humans. The human heart beats, on average, 72 times a minute. The hummingbird's heart beats, on average, 615 times a minute.

THE LANGUAGE OF BIRDS

Birds communicate with one another by a great variety of call notes. There are food calls, danger calls, calls to let their mates and young know where they are, and calls to keep the flock together during migration.

Call notes are signals rather than "words." Young birds inherit their understanding of the notes and produce them when they are needed. Baby chicks become immobile when the mother hen gives a warning note; the shadow of a hawk overhead means danger to the mother, who produces the danger call. The young recognize it and respond with the proper behavior.

FEATHERS

A bird's feathers provide the bird with protection from rain, cold, and heat. A feather has a main shaft that is stiff and solid. A hollow part at the base fits into the bird's skin. Barbs branch from the shaft and together compose the vane. Each barb in turn branches into smaller barbules. Tiny hooks, or hooklets, on the barbules lock all the neighboring barbules together. When a feather is ruffled the wrong way the hooks tear apart. When the feather is smoothed the hooks relock like a zipper.

A colorful toucan.

COLORS AND PATTERN

Every species of bird has its own color and feather pattern. The male and female may look very much alike. The female robin has a brown head and paler breast but otherwise looks like the male. In many species, however, the sexes differ. Usually the male is more brightly colored.

The dull color of most females permits them to remain camouflaged, or protectively colored, and unobserved on the nest. The streaked dark feathers of the female red-winged blackbird blend perfectly with the brown of the nest fastened to the stems of cattails in a marsh. The male, with flashing red and yellow shoulders, perches on top of a cattail some distance away from the nest, drawing all the attention to itself and away from the eggs and young. In the families of birds that nest in holes—for example, the woodpeckers and kingfishers—the females are almost as bright as the males. They do not need to be camouflaged because they and the nest are out of sight.

A kingfisher.

MOLTING

Feathers wear out, as clothes do, and need to be replaced. This change is called molting. All birds molt all their feathers at least once a year, in summer or early fall. Most birds shed only one pair of feathers at a time from wings and tail. The feathers always drop in a definite order. A second pair does not fall until the new pair is almost fully grown. Thus the bird is never handicapped in flying.

A tawny owl.

Ducks, geese, and some other water birds are exceptions. Their flight feathers fall all at once and they are unable to fly. But because they swim, they can find food and hide from their enemies around the edges of waterways.

Can you spot the sand grouse chick?

A flying bird is streamlined like a jet airplane, with its body slender and tapering, but birds are proportionally lighter than planes. All the feathers from head to tail point toward the back of the bird. The wings have delicately curved leading edges and thin trailing edges. The legs of many birds can be drawn up under the body. There are no projecting ears on the head. Even the nostrils in some birds point toward the back of the bird. The air comes out of them like the exhaust from a jet, moving to the rear.

The bones of a bird are light in weight. Many of them are hollow and filled with air. In large soaring birds some of the hollow bones have internal braces like the struts in airplane wings. The frigate bird's wings measure 7 feet (2 meters) or more from tip to tip, yet its skeleton weighs only 4 ounces (113 grams), which is less than the weight of its feathers.

FEATHERED FLIGHT

Descriptive parts of a bird

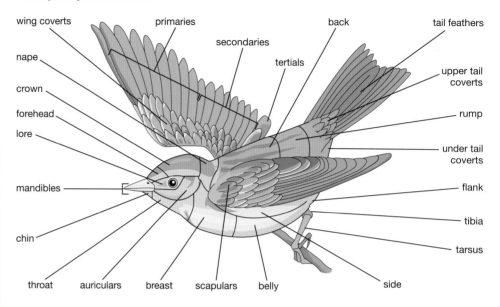

wing coverts · primaries · secondaries · tertials · back · tail feathers · upper tail coverts · rump · under tail coverts · flank · tibia · tarsus · side · belly · scapulars · breast · auriculars · throat · chin · mandibles · lore · forehead · crown · nape

AIR SACS

In addition to having lungs, birds have five or more pairs of air sacs. They are connected to the lungs by small tubes. Branches extend into the hollow bones. The bones of the skull, and sometimes even the small toe bones, are air-filled. The air sacs not only lighten the body but also serve as a cooling system. Birds do not perspire. A constant stream of fresh air flows all through the body by means of the air sacs.

Birds probably never get out of breath. The wing strokes press in the rib case to expel stale air. Hence the faster they fly, the faster the wing muscles pump air and the easier the bird breathes.

FLIGHT FAST FACTS

① The wing feathers most important in pushing a bird forward are the primaries.

② The secondaries are the feathers of the inner wing. They are attached to the lower arm bone. They play an important part in supporting the bird in the air.

③ The tail feathers act as a brake and as a rudder for steering.

④ Most small birds take off with a quick upward leap into the wind and strong fast wing beats. Dabbling, surface-feeding ducks also jump directly from the water. Many water birds, however, have to run over the surface of the water with wings flapping until they gain enough speed to lift themselves into the air.

⑤ Birds land by setting their wings at the proper angle to reduce speed and then throwing the body backward and the legs forward.

MAMMALS

Do the blue whale and the pygmy shrew have anything in common? Despite their size differences, they do: they are both members of a warm-blooded, air-breathing class of vertebrate (backboned) animals known as Mammalia, or mammals. In many ways mammals are the most highly developed of all creatures.

The Class Mammalia contains 29 orders—two orders of monotremes, seven orders of marsupials, and 20 orders of placental mammals. Classification is based on a broad range of characteristics, including anatomy and genetic similarities. Dental characteristics and feeding specializations are also factors in classification.

FIVE FAST FACTS

1 Mammals have existed for the past 200 million years.

2 Mammals evolved from a mammal-like reptile group. These reptile ancestors were small, active carnivores.

3 Mammals have strong lungs.

4 The circulatory system of mammals is very efficient. Their red blood cells can transport more oxygen than those of any other animals, except birds.

5 The mammalian skeletal system has over 200 bones.

MAMMAL CHARACTERISTICS

MILK PRODUCTION

Every female mammal has special glands, mammae, that secrete milk.

VIVIPAROUS

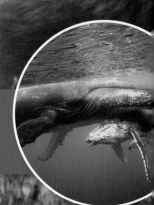

The females of all but the most primitive mammalian species are viviparous. This means they bear their young alive. The young are then fed with milk until they have grown enough to get food for themselves.

HAIR

Hair is a typical mammalian feature. In many whales, however, it exists only in the fetal stages of development.

BRAINS

Mammals have highly developed brains—the most complex known. Particularly well developed is their cerebrum, the part of the brain that controls memory and learning.

BEHAVIORAL ADAPTABILITY

Since the young mammal is dependent on its mother for nourishment, a period of learning is possible. This in turn has brought about a degree of behavioral adaptability unknown in any other group of organisms.

WARM—BLOODED

The term warm-blooded does not mean that a mammal's body temperature is consistently warmer than that of the environment. In the hot tropics, in fact, the opposite is true. Warm-blooded animals, or endotherms, have an inner climate-control system that is physiologically maintained. Mammals can sustain a constant body temperature that is ideal for their bodily functions under most weather conditions.

MONOTREMES

The only mammals that lay eggs, rather than giving birth to live young, are the monotremes. These animals make up the scientific order Monotremata, the most ancient living order of mammals. There are only two kinds of monotreme that survive today: the platypus, which is native to Australia, and the echidnas, found in Australia, New Guinea, and nearby islands.

Platypus.

EGG LAYERS

Monotreme eggs are protected by a soft, leathery shell, like the eggs of reptiles. In both kinds of monotreme, the young break from the egg with the aid of an egg tooth and a fleshy nub called a caruncle, features that are also found in reptiles. When the eggs hatch, the young are relatively undeveloped and completely dependent on their parents. Like other mammals, the monotremes nourish their young with milk produced in mammary glands. Monotremes lack nipples, however; the milk oozes from ducts onto the mother's fur, and the young lap it up.

Echidna.

Australia 25

SPINY ANTEATER

R BATES   R B A

An echidna's spines.

FIVE FAST FACTS

1. The adult male platypus is slightly larger than the female and has hollow spurs connected to venom glands on the ankle of each hind leg. The poison, while not fatal to humans, can be quite painful. The spurs are used in combat when males fight to protect their territory and to determine which of them will mate with the females.

2. When reports from Australia of this animal's existence first reached Europe in the late 1700s, scientists dismissed the platypus as a hoax.

3. Although bizarre in appearance, the platypus is perfectly adapted to its semiaquatic life in lakes and streams. It is an excellent swimmer and diver and is able to stay submerged for up to five minutes.

4. Also called spiny anteaters, echidnas have dome-shaped bodies that are covered with spines as well as fur. The spines protect these animals from predators.

5. An echidna uses its long sticky tongue to catch ants, termites, worms, and other invertebrates.

MARSUPIALS

Mammals that carry their young in an abdominal pouch during their early development are called marsupials. Soon after the marsupial ovum, or egg, is fertilized, the young are born in a premature state and crawl into the mother's pouch. There, nursing on milk from their mother's nipples, they complete their development. Common marsupials include the kangaroos and koalas of Australia and New Guinea, the Tasmanian devil of Tasmania, and the opossums of North and South America.

THE LARGEST AND SMALLEST

The largest living marsupials are the red and gray kangaroos of Australia. Males of these species reach lengths of about 5 feet (1.5 meters) from the nose to the tip of the tail. The average weight of large males ranges from 110 to as much as 200 pounds (50 to 90 kilograms). Females, however, are smaller.

The smallest marsupials are species of the marsupial mice, or planigales, which grow to an average length of less than 4 inches (10 centimeters) and weigh only about two tenths of an ounce (6 grams).

WHERE THEY ARE FOUND

Australia, New Guinea, and Tasmania are the strongholds of many marsupials, including the kangaroos, wombats, phalangers, and bandicoots. More than a dozen families and about 175 species are known to inhabit this part of the world.

The other major region where marsupials occur is in the tropical parts of South and Central America, where more than 80 species of opossums live. With the exception of a few species that may enter Northern Mexico, a single marsupial species, the Virginia opossum, is found in North America.

FIVE FAST FACTS

1 Fossils indicate that some ancient Australian marsupials were as large as elephants.

2 In many marsupial species the hind limbs are larger and better developed than the forelimbs.

3 The tail is often well developed and may be used for support or grasping.

4 After marsupial young are weaned, they begin roaming for short distances and eating food on their own. The young of many species, however, remain with the mother for some time after weaning, sometimes returning to her pouch in search of rest or protection.

5 Most marsupial pouches open toward the front, but those of the koalas and bandicoots open to the rear. Males normally have no pouch.

A koala mother with its young joey.

Wombats.

Bandicoot.

A mother opossum carries her babies.

RODENTS

Probably more than half of the mammals living on Earth are rodents. Rodents, gnawing animals of the order Rodentia, are found on all the major landmasses except Antarctica and on most islands. The order includes various species of rats and mice, squirrels, chipmunks, voles, gerbils, hamsters, lemmings, beavers, pocket gophers, guinea pigs, and porcupines.

A squirrel gnawing on a walnut.

THESE TEETH ARE MADE FOR GNAWING

Although they appear in many diverse forms, all rodents have the same kind of jaws and incisors. When the hinged lower jaw is pulled back, the grinding, or cheek, teeth come into contact for grinding food; when the jaw is pulled forward and down, the tips of the large upper and lower incisors meet for gnawing. These incisors grow throughout the animal's life. If they are not used enough they will grow past each other and eventually cause the animal's death, either by making the rodent incapable of eating or by actually growing back into the skull.

Capybaras are the largest of the rodents.

Chinchillas are valued for their fur.

Some mammal orders are based on common feeding specializations. More than 450 species of shrews, moles, tenrecs, and hedgehogs are divided among three orders of small insectivorous (insect-eating) mammals.

INSECTIVORES

The mole spends most of its life in darkness. It lives in an underground burrow and tunnels through soil to find its food of earthworms and other invertebrates.

MOLES

SHREWS

Small and mouselike, shrews are among the most abundant mammals in the world. Shrews are extremely nervous and sensitive. The heart may beat 1,200 times per minute, and a shrew may die from the shock of a rough touch or a loud noise.

The hedgehog sleeps by day, and at night it pokes and burrows in the ground, feeding on such food as insects, frogs, and occasionally small mammals.

HEDGEHOGS

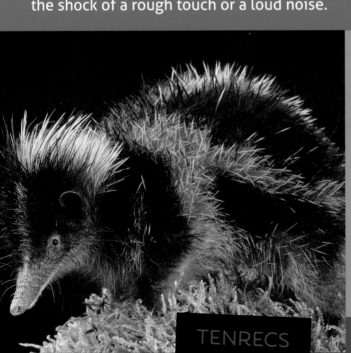

TENRECS

Tenrecs, found natively to Madagascar and Comoros Islands, are typically round-bodied, big-headed animals with pointed faces and very wide mouths when opened.

BATS

More than 1,200 species of bats are currently classified in the order Chiroptera. They have soft fur and large ears, and as babies they drink milk from their mothers. They are distinguished by their ability to navigate at night by using a system of sound vibrations (echolocation). This allows them to chase insects through thick forests on the darkest night without striking a branch or twig.

WHERE THEY LIVE

Bats are found throughout the world except in the cold polar regions. They are particularly abundant in rainforests and jungles. The United States is known to have 40 species of bats. They mostly live in the southwestern states, where the weather is relatively warm year-round.

Bats are shy animals and will try to avoid humans. They are active at night and spend the day sleeping in out-of-the-way places, such as in caves or on high branches. They often rest together in colonies, or large groups, for extra protection and to keep warm.

FIVE FAST FACTS

1 The largest bats have a wingspan of about 5 feet (1.5 meters) and a weight of about 2.2 pounds (1 kilogram).

2 One of the smallest bats has a wingspan of barely 6 inches (15 centimeters) and weighs about 0.07 ounce (about 2 grams).

3 Though flight speeds in the wild are hard to measure, some species have been timed on average at 11.7 to 20.8 miles (18.7 to 33.3 kilometers) per hour.

4 While flying, bats can control each of the four fingers of the wing separately.

5 The thumb, always free of the wing, is used for walking or climbing in some species; in others it is used for handling food.

A bat eating fruit.

WHAT THEY EAT

Most bats eat insects. Other bats feed on fruits. Others eat large insects, spiders, and scorpions that they find on the ground, on walls, or on vegetation. Several types of bats are meat-eaters, feeding on small rodents, shrews, bats, sleeping birds, tree frogs, and lizards. A few even catch and eat small fish. Vampire bats, which feed on the blood of large mammals or birds, bite an animal's skin until the blood flows freely and then lick the blood with their tongue.

CARNIVORES

The highly diverse order Carnivora ("meat-eaters") contains more than 270 species, including the canines (dogs and related species), felines (large and small cats), raccoons, bears, weasels, skunks, otters, and many others. Over time some of the Carnivora adopted a broader diet. For example, raccoons and bears are omnivorous and include fruits and other plant foods in their diet. The giant panda has become completely herbivorous, consuming only plant matter. The aquatic pinnipeds (seals, sea lions, and walruses) also belong to Carnivora.

WOLVES

Wolves generally travel in packs and frequently establish territories ranging from 40 to more than 400 square miles (100 to 1,000 square kilometers). They define their ranges with scent markings and such vocalizations as growls, barks, and their legendary howl.

POLAR BEAR

The most carnivorous of bears, the polar bear lives on ice far from land and on coastal areas and islands of the Arctic Ocean. Its long, thick white fur and a thick layer of fat help keep it warm. The fur on the soles of its feet helps it walk on ice.

RACCOONS

Raccoons swim and climb readily. They often live together high in hollow trees or sometimes in rock crevices, stumps, or other animals' burrows.

WEASELS

Weasels are bold and aggressive predators. They generally hunt alone and principally eat mice, voles, rats, and rabbits, but they also consume frogs, birds, and bird eggs. Because of their narrow bodies, weasels are able to pursue and capture rodents in their burrows and are able to chase them through holes and crevices, under dense foliage, up trees, or into water.

CATS

All cats move in the same way. They walk on the tips of their toes, not on the soles of their feet as do humans and many other kinds of animals.

UNGULATES

The hoofed herbivorous (plant-eating) mammals commonly called ungulates are classified with several related groups in the grandorder Ungulata. This large and diverse group includes more than 300 species divided among seven orders.

The artiodactyls—hoofed ungulates with an even number of toes—make up the largest order in the Ungulata. Cows, deer, pigs, sheep, giraffes, and camels are part of this group. The perissodactyls—odd-toed ungulates such as horses, zebras, tapirs, and rhinoceroses—form a smaller order. Closely related to these two groups but classified in their own order are the elephants. The grandorder also includes manatees and their relatives, hyraxes, and cetaceans (whales, porpoises, and dolphins). Many cetaceans are omnivorous. The smallest order in the Ungulata contains a single species—the aardvark, which is insectivorous.

GIRAFFES

The giraffe is the tallest of all living land animals. Males, called bulls, may exceed 18 feet (5.5 meters) in height, and the tallest females, called cows, are about 15 feet (4.5 meters).

CAMELS

The two species of large hoofed animals known as camels were domesticated about 4,000 to 5,000 years ago. Ever since, they have provided meat, milk, wool, and hides to various desert- and mountain-dwelling peoples of the Eastern and Western Hemispheres.

TAPIRS

Tapirs live in swamps and near the streams of jungle forests. They are solitary, night-feeding animals, sleeping by day hidden among the foliage near the river's edge. When pursued, they take to the water if possible, for they swim well.

ELEPHANTS

When elephants meet, one may touch the face of the other, or they will intertwine trunks. This "trunk-shake" can be compared to a human handshake.

AARDVARKS

Aardvarks feed by night and sleep in underground burrows by day. They have powerful front legs, armed with four strong claws on each forefoot. With these claws they tear open termite mounds that humans can break into only with a pickax. Their tough skin protects them from the bites of soldier termites.

PRIMATES

The most-advanced mammals are the primates, which include the lemurs, lorises, tarsiers, monkeys, apes, and humans. There are more than 300 species in the order Primates, making it one of the largest and most-diverse mammalian orders. Primates have well-developed hands, keen, stereoscopic vision, and a large brain. Most nonhuman primates use all four limbs for locomotion; some monkey species have a long, prehensile, or grasping, tail that acts as a fifth limb.

LEMURS

The name lemur comes from the Latin word *lemures*, meaning "ghosts." It was given to these animals because of the silent, ghostlike way they move about. Although some lemurs are active during the day, the observers who assigned the name probably witnessed the eerily shining eyes of nocturnal species.

LORISES

Lorises live in trees and rarely go down to the ground. They usually move slowly with hand-over-hand deliberateness on the top and along the underside of limbs. They often hang by their feet, leaving their hands free to grasp food or branches. Lorises spend their days rolled up in a tight ball, asleep. When night arrives, they start searching for food.

TARSIERS

Tarsiers are small, nocturnal primates native to the Southeast Asian islands of Philippines, Celebes, Borneo, and Sumatra. They have long legs, short bodies, elongated digits with rounded adhesive pads, and rounded heads that can rotate 180 degrees. They cling vertically to trees and leap from trunk to trunk.

MONKEYS

Like the apes, most monkeys have opposable thumbs and great toes. In addition, some species have a prehensile, or grasping, tail, which they use to cling to branches. Color vision, acute hearing, and some form of vocalization are also characteristic of monkeys.

APES

The apes are usually divided into two subgroups: the lesser apes—gibbons— and the great apes—orangutans, chimpanzees, and gorillas. These animals share many characteristics, but each is quite distinctive in appearance and lifestyle. From the acrobatic gibbon to the resourceful chimpanzee, and from the solitary orangutan to the family-oriented gorilla, the apes are a diverse and intriguing lot.

MIGRATIONS

Many people take trips periodically, often seasonally, in search of a fair climate, good food, and a change of scene in pleasant surroundings. Some animals are impelled to travel for similar reasons, and their trips, too, are often annual and linked to the seasons. These traveling animals are called migrants and their trips, migrations.

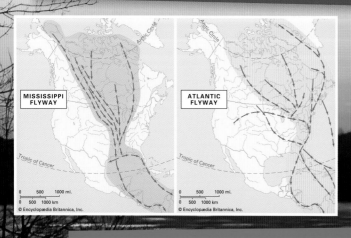

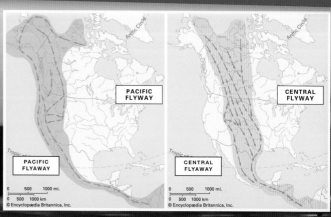

These maps show migration routes by different types of birds. A flyway is a broader area where many migration routes converge.

WHAT ANIMALS MIGRATE?

Most kinds of migrant animals make the round trip each year. Grazing animals, particularly the hoofed animals of Eastern Africa and the Arctic tundra, follow the seasonal changes in their supplies of green plants. Even fishes move about according to the season. Eels and many salmon make a round-trip only once in their life cycle. These animals return to the home waters where they were born to lay their eggs, and then they usually die.

Some animals make long journeys back and forth across land and ocean. Other migrations, however, take a vertical direction. During seasons of severe weather in mountainous regions, for instance, certain birds, insects, and mammals make regular trips down from the high altitudes where they breed into the foothills or plains below.

HOW DO ANIMALS NAVIGATE?

Although they have no maps or compasses to guide them, many animals find their way over long distances. Animals use mountains, rivers, coasts, vegetation, and even climatic conditions such as prevailing winds to orient themselves. Even fishes use topographical clues to recognize their underwater range. Birds have been seen to hesitate and explore as they search for recognizable landmarks.

Birds can see ultraviolet light. They can also hear very low-frequency sound caused by wind blowing over ocean waves and mountains thousands of miles away. Many birds also possess a compass sense. They are able to fly in a particular, constant direction. Furthermore, they can tell in which direction to go in order to get home. They use the sun to get their bearings. Certain insects—bees, for example—do not even need to see the sun itself. They respond to the polarization of sunlight (which humans cannot detect) and orient themselves by the pattern it forms in a blue sky, even when the sun is behind the clouds.

ANIMAL SENSES

All animals have the ability to sense and respond to their surroundings. The more highly developed animals have sense organs to perceive light, sound, touch, taste, and smell.

VISION

Eyes are very important to most mammals. Animals that hunt and feed by night have very large eyes. The eyes of cats and some nocturnal animals have pupils that can open wide in the dark and narrow down to slits in the sunlight. Insects have compound eyes, made up of tiny units that break up the image into many small images. They also have two or three simple eyes that probably detect motion. The eyesight of some fish is especially keen.

HEARING

Ears are perhaps as important as eyes to some species. The fennec is a foxlike animal that lives in the Sahara and hunts by night. Its large ears help it detect its prey in the darkness of a hot, dry climate, where food may be very scarce. The cat is also a night prowler, and it too has large, erect ears. The hearing organs of the field cricket and katydid are located on their forelegs. The organ is a thin membrane that vibrates in response to sound waves.

TOUCH

The barbels of the catfish and the whiskers of the flying squirrel and the domestic cat are organs of touch. They are very useful for animals that explore in the dark. The lateral line of the fish is a rod of nerve cells running the length of the body. It probably helps fish sense movements in the surrounding water.

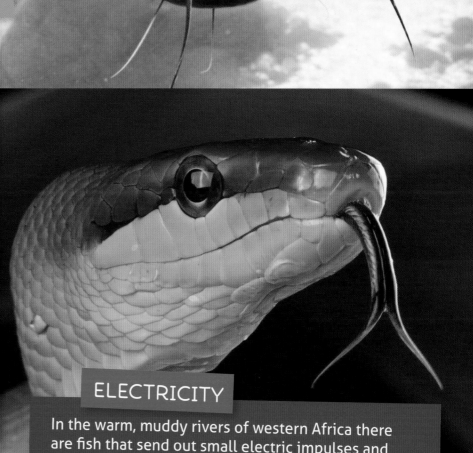

OTHER SENSES AND SENSE ORGANS

Many animals have sense organs that are different from those of mammals. The antennae of moths, butterflies, and other insects are the organs of taste, touch, smell, and hearing.

The delicate forked tongue of the snake tastes the air. With it the snake can locate food and other snakes. The rattlesnake has sensory pits on the head that can detect the infrared radiation, or heat, from nearby animals, enabling it to locate potential prey in the dark.

ELECTRICITY

In the warm, muddy rivers of western Africa there are fish that send out small electric impulses and surround themselves with an electric field. The fish is made aware of the approach of other organisms by changes in the electric field. This system therefore takes the place of eyesight in the dark waters and keeps the fish informed of its surroundings.

PREDATOR AND PREY

Animals must eat, either directly or indirectly, the food manufactured by producer organisms. A horse cannot stand in the sun and wait for its body to make carbohydrates and proteins. It must move around the pasture in search of green grass. Even meat eaters—for example, lions—live on animals, such as zebras, which in turn subsist on plants. Animals that eat other animals are called carnivores. Animals that feed on insects are known as insectivores. A large group of animals are herbivores, which means they eat producer organisms, namely plants and algae. Many herbivores are prey of the carnivores. Animals that eat both animal and plant matter are referred to as omnivores.

DEFENSES

All animals have some means of defending themselves against enemies. A cat can usually outrun a dog and climb the nearest tree. If cornered, it will scratch and bite.

Many animals rely on speed, camouflage, teeth, claws, and even intimidation to escape other animals. The variety of means of protection is extensive. Porcupines and hedgehogs roll into a ball and raise their sharp quills. The quills come off and stick into the nose or paw of an unwary dog or some other enemy. Skunks spray a foul-smelling fluid from a gland when they are frightened. Deer, moose, and antelope fight with their antlers. Squids shoot out a cloud of inky material and escape under its cover. The electric ray and several other kinds of fish have built-in electric storage cells by which they can deliver a paralyzing shock. Some insects, snakes, and lizards protect themselves with their venom. Many amphibians produce poisonous skin secretions.

PROTECTIVE COLORATION

As animals evolved, most of them developed body colors and markings that improved their chances of surviving. This adaptive mechanism, known as protective coloration, may serve any number of functions.

Coloring can help protect an animal by making it hard to see. For an animal that spends much of its life trying to avoid dangerous enemies, this is the most useful function.

Conversely, color can help an organism by making it more conspicuous—the bright colors of a poisonous snake may warn off intruders, for example. In general, the purpose of protective coloration is to decrease an organism's visibility or to alter its appearance to other organisms.

Do you see the spider?

 LEARN MORE ABOUT CAMOUFLAGE AND COLORATION IN THE APP!

A lioness pursues zebras.

SOCIAL BEHAVIOR

All living things relate to other members of their species. In an amoeba, the relationship occurs only during the short time it takes the animal to split into two animals. In other species, such as the social insects, the relationship is so necessary that they cannot survive as individuals. Social organization of some kind is common to all animals. However, the type of organization varies with the nervous system of the species. And in true social organization, animals of the same species react to each other.

Prairie dogs establish elaborate social organizations.

SIMPLE SYSTEMS

Organisms with relatively simple systems may respond to each other only as long as they give off attractive or offensive stimuli. For example, a goby will remain near its eggs only as long as the hormonal state of the fish and the chemical and visual features of the eggs remain the same. Once the fry, or young, hatch, the fish responds to them as it would toward any small fish and tries to eat them. The goby does not recognize the fry as its own offspring.

DOMINANCE

In communities of certain animals the ruling, or dominant, animal is the largest, strongest, or most aggressive and thereby exerts the most influence on the other animals in the group. The dominant animal enjoys the greatest and most preferential access to members of the opposite sex and control of the best territory for feeding and breeding. Scientists have found that many groups of animals, most notably baboons, birds, foxes, lions, and crocodiles, establish dominance hierarchies. The best-known example is the pecking order of chickens. Flock members are arranged on the "rungs" of a social ladder, with each chicken superior to those below and subordinate to those above.

Chickens squabble for dominance.

COMMUNICATION

Communication in the animal world takes many forms. These include chemical, visual, and audible signals. Attacked insects secrete a pheromone that so excites their conspecifics that they either attack or escape from the predator. Flocks of birds behave similarly, except that sounds rather than chemicals trigger the response. Vocalization also evokes social responses in the porpoise, an aquatic mammal. Porpoises communicate by means of whistles and other sounds.

A troop of monkeys.

BANDS

Some birds and many mammals band in large groups, such as herds and families. These groups include adult males and females and offspring of different ages. The offspring in most mammalian groups remain with the group until they reach sexual maturity. The females frequently remain until the group splits up. Some socially bonded groups of mammals consist of an older male, a number of younger males, many females, and immature offspring. Among the howler monkeys, the younger males band together into a marginal bachelor group until each establishes himself as the older male in a new social group.

DOMESTICATION

The human race's progress on Earth has been due in part to the animals that people have been able to utilize throughout history. Such domesticated animals carry people and their burdens. They pull machinery and help cultivate fields. They provide food and clothing. As pets they may amuse or console their owners.

Domesticated animals are those that have been bred in captivity for many generations. While a single animal may be tamed, only a species of animals can be considered domesticated. In the course of time, by selective breeding, certain animals have changed greatly in appearance and behavior from their wild ancestors. There is a vast difference between the scrawny red jungle fowl of southern Asia and its descendant, the heavy-breasted, egg-laying farm chicken.

Przhevalski's horses have not been domesticated.

The Inca in Peru were the first to domesticate llamas and alpacas.

FIVE FAST FACTS

1 There seems to be little doubt that the dog was the first animal domesticated by humans. Its bones are common in campsites of the late Neolithic that date back more than 10,000 years.

2 Beginning in about 8000 BC and continuing over a period of about 5,000 years, all the other animals important to humans today were domesticated. Remains of cattle, sheep, and pigs have been found among Mesopotamian ruins dating from some time before 3000 BC.

3 Not one new species has been domesticated in the past 4,000 years, unless laboratory animals such as mice, rats, and monkeys can be considered domesticated.

4 The horse was the last important animal to be domesticated. The only species of wild horse still living are Przhevalski's horse, very small numbers of which survive in the wild in western Mongolia, and the Riwoche horse, a few of which survive in northeastern Tibet.

5 Unsuccessful attempts at domestication have been made with the bison, related to cattle; with the zebra, related to the horse; and with the peccary, a cousin of the pig.

Northern Europeans first domesticated the reindeer.

A domesticated pig and its cousin, the wild boar.

EVOLUTION AND ADAPTATION

Evolution is the theory that all the kinds of living things that exist today developed from earlier types. The differences between them resulted from changes that happened over many years. The simplest forms of life arose at least 3.5 billion years ago. Over time they evolved into the millions of species, or types, of living things alive today.

Nearly all scientists accept evolution. This theory is central to the modern science of biology. As a scientific theory, evolution is testable. Scientists have performed many experiments and examined huge amounts of evidence from a variety of scientific fields. The evidence very strongly supports evolution.

WHAT IS NATURAL SELECTION?

The theory of natural selection is based on the idea that living things are in constant competition for limited but essential resources in their environment, such as food and shelter. Organisms with traits that help them or their offspring survive, which are known as adaptations, have an advantage over those with harmful or less useful traits. In the struggle for existence, the better-adapted organisms are selected and thrive at the expense of their competition. The more successful animals reproduce and pass their adaptive traits to their offspring while those that are not as well adapted have fewer offspring and eventually die out.

Charles Darwin was the father of the modern theory of evolution.

Evolution of a horse.

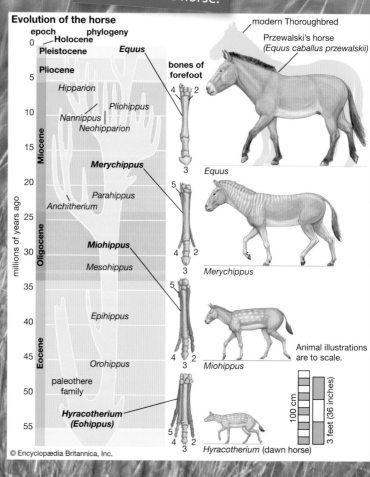

Evolution of the horse

epoch   phylogeny

© Encyclopædia Britannica, Inc.

ADAPTATION

Many animals have adaptations that help them elude their predators. The brownish color of a deer's coat blends with its woodland surroundings, making it difficult for a predator to spot it. The deer's behavior, too, is adaptive: deer remain absolutely still when they perceive that a threat is near.

Predators have adaptations that help them capture prey. The lion's tawny coat, the tiger's stripes, and the spotted fur of other big cats help camouflage these predators in their respective habitats, making it difficult for prey to see them. The cheetah's great speed results from several adaptations: its legs are proportionally longer than those of other big cats, it has special paw pads for extra traction, and its long tail affords it extra balance. The heart and respiratory system are relatively large, increasing the cheetah's capacity to move oxygen through the body, further fueling its capacity to reach and sustain high speeds.

FIND OUT MORE ABOUT CAMOUFLAGE IN THE VR APP.

The peppered moth blends in with bark. When tree bark became darker due to factory soot, the moths became darker as well.

EXTINCTION

The permanent disappearance or elimination of a species is called extinction. This generally occurs when a species is unable to adapt to a change in its environment. That is, when the environment changes, species that lack the characteristics that would allow them to thrive in their new circumstances are likely to go extinct.

Scientists divide extinction events into two categories based on the scale of the event—background extinctions and mass extinctions.

The worst mass extinction event was the Permian extinction, which occurred about 266 million to 251 million years ago. About 95 percent of marine species were lost.

BACKGROUND EXTINCTIONS

The ongoing extinction of individual species because of environmental factors is known collectively as background extinctions. Background extinctions are part of the natural cycle of life on Earth. Habitat loss, changes in the food supply, the introduction of a new predator or an invasive species, severe climatic events such as droughts or extended flooding, natural disasters such as hurricanes or volcanic eruptions—all of these are factors that can make it difficult for species to survive. When such an event changes one or more factors in the environment, some species may not be adapted to handle the change in their surroundings. Background extinctions usually affect one or several species that inhabit a small area, such as a forest or a lake.

dodo
(*Raphus cucullatus*)

mamo
(*Drepanis pacifica*)

passenger pigeon
(*Ectopistes migratorius*)

Tasmanian wolf
(*Thylacinus cynocephalus*)

© Encyclopædia Britannica, Inc.

MASS EXTINCTIONS

The primary difference between background extinctions and mass extinctions is scale. Whereas background extinctions may involve a few species that inhabit a small area, mass extinction events result in the demise of vast numbers of species over a very large geographic area, even globally. Scientific evidence suggests that mass extinctions occur as a result of catastrophic events such as an asteroid impact or ice age.

Extinction occurring on such a vast scale requires a disaster of considerable proportion, and such disasters have been relatively rare during Earth's history. The fossil record provides evidence for five mass extinction events that have occurred over the past 600 million years.

THE SIXTH MASS EXTINCTION?

In modern times, many species have become extinct because of human activities, particularly the destruction of natural environments. Current rates of human-induced extinctions are estimated to be about 1,000 times greater than past natural background rates of extinction. This has led some scientists to call modern times the sixth mass extinction.

Animals at risk of dying out are called endangered species. The black rhinoceros is endangered.

TEST WHAT YOU KNOW

1. Which animal is not an herbivore?

   Elephant   Shrew

   Goat   Giraffe

2. There are more invertebrate species than vertebrate species on Earth.

   True   False

3. Reptiles like snakes are the only animals that molt, or shed their skin.

   True   False

4. Invertebrates can only grow to a length of about a foot because they do not have a backbone to support them.

   True   False

5. Vertebrates are warm-blooded.

   True   False

6. The order Urodela contains:

   Snakes   Salamanders

   Turtles   Frogs

7. Scientists believe reptiles successfully made the leap to land because of this characteristic.

   The ability to shed their skin

   The ability to hibernate

   Amniotic eggs   Venom

8. These adaptations help a bird to fly.

   Air sacs   A streamlined body

   Hollow bones   All of these

Answers: 1. Shrews are insectivores; 2. True; 3. False. Amphibians and arthropods molt as well; 4. False. Land invertebrates stay small, but invertebrates in water, such as large squids, can grow to great lengths; 5. False. Mammals and birds are warm-blooded, but fish, amphibians, and reptiles are not; 6. Salamanders; 7. Amniotic eggs; 8. All of these.

6 MONTHS FREE

ENCYCLOPÆDIA
Britannica ONLINE©

This certificate entitles you to use
Encyclopædia Britannica Online© **FREE FOR 6 MONTHS!**

Your subscription will begin on the day you activate your account by following these simple instructions:

1. Access the online registration form provided at: **www.britannica.com/certificate**
2. Enter the Promotion Code that appears below.
3. Follow the steps to create your password and account profile.

Promotion Code: | EBVR2017 | Codes must be redeemed by:
December 31, 2021

TROUBLESHOOTING

The image I see is blurry.

Make sure the smartphone is aligned precisely with the center of the viewer.
Adjusting the phone left or right a few millimeters can make a big difference.
The tilt of the viewer and the phone can also affect how the screen looks to you.
You can also try to calibrate the viewer using one of the QR codes found below.

I was asked to allow the app to take pictures.
Do I need to allow this?

Yes, this allows the app to take a picture of the QR code in your book in
order to validate your purchase and access the accompanying app.

How do I calibrate my viewer?

If asked to calibrate your viewer, scan the first of the QR codes found below. If the picture seems
blurry afterward, touch the small gear icon that appears at one corner of your screen. You will
then be given an opportunity to Switch Viewers. Scan the other QR code found here. Some
smartphones work better with one calibration, while others work better with the second.

I'm getting a pop-up that this app won't work without Google VR Services,
asking me to install it before continuing. Do I need to do this?

Click Cancel; it should not prevent you from running the app successfully.

Can I use this viewer with other apps?

The viewer is a standard size that is designed to be compatible with many apps. Try it out!

I damaged my viewer. Can I use this app with other viewers?

Yes, this app is compatible with many other standard-sized viewers on the market.

My screen gets dim when I place it in the viewer.

Check your phone settings. Under Display settings, if there is a setting such as "Auto adjust
brightness," where the screen adapts to lighting conditions, turn that setting off.